I0213592

Screams From The Heart of A Woman

By
Marva Collins-Bush

Copyright ©2010 by Marva Collins-Bush

All rights reserved. This book may not be reproduced in whole or in part, stored in a retrieval system, or transmitted in any form or any means – electronic, mechanical or other – without written permission from the publisher, except by a reviewer who may quote brief passages in a review.

Louisianachic Publishing
P.O. Box 444
Bastrop, LA 71221

Dust Jacket Design on Lulu.com

ISBN 978-0-578-05485-8

DEDICATION

This second edition for:

Tamala, Cathon and Jomal, the souls of my heart.

Acknowledgements

Katherine Miller, Alice Miller, Walter Brandon and all the residents of Henry Street/Avenue between Pearl St. and South Haggerty St/Martin Luther King South in Bastrop, Louisiana during the years of 1946-1964.

My life is rich because of you. You gave me a new story to tell every day. I jumped out of bed daily to see what new adventures you would put before me in that twenty-four hour period. Your living gave me something to look forward to back then as it does today.

Thank you for the lessons, thank you for the experiences and thank you for the rich meaningful stories I tell today.

Screams From the Heart of Woman

This is your book too. Write your thoughts, poems or anything you'd like on the blank pages

BETRAYAL

I told you things I never

told anyone

and

you took those secret

places of my soul

and used them against me.

You went after my man

like you had a homing

device in the center of

your brain.

What you forgot though

is that

he is my man,

and remains,

my man.

CHEAT

I Saw The Two Of You

I Saw You Smile At Her

I Saw Your Arms Around Her

I Saw Her Smile At You

I Saw Your Happiness

I Saw Me Cry.

GONE

You ran through my life

without a "fine thank you"

I dreamed dreams,

Envisioned visions

About us

And

About you

And about me

And

About we.

The choirs sang,

The gods smiled,

I snuggled in for a

Lifetime of love and laughter.

ABRUPTLY

You were gone,

Without a conjunction,

A comma or

A hyphen.

ABRUPTLY

You were gone.

Period.

MY TIME

It's my time now.

Play by my rules

or not at all.

Satisfy me

or move on.

Respect me

or forget it.

Dance by my music

or hire your own band

Love me

or leave me alone

It's my time now.

ME

Black Berry

Hershey Bar

Chocolate child

Mmmm Mmmm

Good.

SELFISH

We've got

one thing

in common.

I love you

and

you love you.

JADED

I look at the

ashes that

used to be your

manhood

and I am so lonely.

Your manhood, your self.

Your you,

snatched and

reduced to ashes.

I see the rage that spills

out on me.

Me,

the receptacle for

your rage.

So long,

It's gone on

for so long.

I confuse brutality

with love.

bitch with sweetheart,

struggle with happiness

pain with joy

hate with tenderness.

I can't receive your

rage today.

Your rage mixed

with mine.

My love, my beaten,

jaded love.

I have a rage of

my own.

My enslavement was

the same as yours.

My mental rape is

the same as yours,

we struggle, we rant,

we rage.

And my rage

destroy you as

yours does me.

The ashes that

used to be

you.

The ashes that used

to be

me

Trying, screaming

to get back to

the love.

Faces, numerous

faces, all the

same, full of

rage.

This time, I know

it will be different.

It isn't.

The rage is all

consuming.

I cry for the

innocence lost.

The love lost.

My man,

my beautiful

Black man.

So full of love

but the rage

gets in the

way.

The brutality

is all that we have…

Until the love

returns.

EGO

It's a waste to

become self-satisfied

because you

know who

you are.

Get up and

act it out!

FREE TO LOVE YOU

I don't want to

fight you anymore.

I just want to

remember how to care.

Remember how to touch you

with the touch

that touches.

The fight is over.

The war is done.

No victor,

just two victims.

I don't want to fight

you anymore.

I don't want to struggle

apart.

I want to struggle

together,

to

crawl together

to

stand together

to

walk together

to

run together

to

soar together

to

win together.

I don't want to fight you

anymore

I just don't want to

fight you anymore.

BLACK MAN

Head up!

Shoulders back!

Stomach in!

Thighs taunt!

Strides long!

Strut your

Kingly step!!!

DECEPTION

You stood there

and watched me

fall in love with

you.

You did nothing to

stop me.

All the time you

knew you'd never

love me

and

you stood there and

watched me

fall in love with

you.

BETRAYAL II

This is my man

I already know that.

Your beauty intimidated me,

But this is my man.

Your talent sent waves of

burning envy through me,

But yet, he is my man.

You can't have him

because

he is mine.

The trust,

the love,

the beauty,

the joy,

the sharing,

the giving

it's all mine.

Go get your own.

I still love you, Sister of mine.

But, he's my man.

YOU AND ME

How can I say it?

I love you seems so trite.

You noticed when no one else did.

You saw it.

You saw through me.

You saw the façade.

You loved me and asked

nothing in return.

Not even a kiss.

You never came on to me.

You just loved me,

Just as I am.

Sparks flew when we met.

You were my completion.

The other half of me…

but only for a time.

Then we moved on,

with no sorrow and

no regrets.

No bad memories,

just two people who

cared deeply

for each other.

WE

My completion,

The other side of me,

the other side of you.

I am as close to you

as your skin.

When your heart beat,

I beat.

I am you and you are me.

It was meant to

be that way.

Run, run from you,

For what?

The things I run from,

I run to.

For

I am closer than

your skin.

When your heart beat,

I beat.

The fear,

the waiting,

the anguish,

all a part of it.

The coming into being

of me and you.

The birth of

the we.

I am pregnant with us.

Will I have this we

or

Will I abort?

I've aborted so many We/Us

The fear,

the waiting,

the anguish

makes it so.

Will I have this We/Us

or

Will I abort?

LONGEVITY

Longevity!

Get the heck out of the mind game called

longevity

What does it matter

that we've spent

fourteen years of our

lives together?

You don't know me

and I don't know you.

We got caught up in

staying together.

We never learned to be together.

Longevity equaled stability.

Longevity for the kids.

Longevity for our parents.

Longevity for our friends.

Never about you and me.

Longevity, Yeah!

Get the heck out of the

mind game, called longevity.

YOU ARE MY SISTER

Girl, let me tell you something.

listen to me.

I hear you talking,

jaws just flapping in the wind.

You say

I'm not putting up with this.

I'm not taking that.

Ain't nobody gonna make a

fool outta me.

I don't need nobody.

I can take care of myself.

but

I see your eyes.

I see your sad eyes,

Only inches above your

brave smile.

I see your eyes.

Did you ever stop to think

that maybe the reason,

the reason

your bed is empty

is because you won't

take this

and you won't put up with that

and

you ain't gonna let

nobody make a fool outta you.

Your sisters, they lie.

They lie to you.

They say they've got it all

under control.

It confuses you that theirs

is so together and

yours is so ragged.

They lie girl, they lie.

They're compromising and

sacrificing and

all the stuff

They tell you not to do,

They are all doing.

anything and everything

to keep their thing together.

Wake up!

You've been sleep too long.

Wake up!

LONELY PEOPLE

A world of lonely people

unable to commit,

trying anything but

commitment.

Trying everything but

commitment.

Games, games, games.

Stop the games.

How?

Gaming so long,

gaming since forever.

Stop the games

and love.

Commit!

FOUND

Your tenderness,

Your softness,

I lean into it

and you allow it.

I expected you to run

and you stood your ground.

The pressure overwhelms me.

they always run.

They never stand.

Where did you come from

with your tenderness and

your softness?

My rough edges smooth

against your softness.

I am lost and

found at once.

The games of the past

Are ineffective.

I am lost and

Found at once.

The dreams deep

Within me

Come true.

I am found.

FRIENDS

We were friends.

I could count on you.

When you hugged me,

I knew you cared.

We talked for hours on end

about nothing.

We communicated.

We touched in the most

intimate way.

Spirit to Spirit

Soul to Soul

Mind to Mind.

I covered for you..

You covered for me...

We beat the system..

Together we were a team.

Why did you have to ruin it?

Why did you have to say

you desired me?

I didn't need another lover,

I needed a friend.

LOST

What am I doing this for?

Why do I stay?

Why don't I take my

Change of clothes

And go?

It began because of

My love for you and

The love I thought you had for me.

The love is gone,

The memory of it too.

All that is left is

The bitterness

The fighting

The struggle.

Love let me go.

Take your bittersweet

Shackles off me.

I am helpless,

tied to what was and

what could have been.

What good am I?

You said you have no

room in your life for

a person with nothing.

Well, I am now that person.

I have nothing.

STRENGTH

Don't envy my strength

use it.

I only have it

to share with you.

Trust my strength

to take you

where you are going.

Don't be afraid

of it.

My strength will not

devour you.

It only seems that way.

It is yours for

the asking.

I am only the

guardian of the strength.

It truly belongs

to you.

You are my strength's

rightful owner.

When you are ready

to claim it

My strength is

rightfully yours.

WAITING

Waiting…

Is there anything harder to do?

Waiting requires patience.

I have so little.

How does one stand still?

How do you stop the wheels

of your mind from turning?

Is it possible to wait and not trip?

Who said patience is a virtue?

If it is so virtuous,

why is it so hard?

Nothing worth having comes

Without effort.

Waiting takes effort. Lots of effort.

When will my turn come?

Sometimes it seems as if the

waiting will be for nothing.

It will all turn out to be

some big joke on me.

The jester jumps out of

the shadows and

laughs at me.

"The joke is on you. The joke is on you, you fool."

The scary stories in the dark recesses

of my mind

frighten me in the middle of the night.

A chorus of tormentors play havoc

in my innermost being

in the still of the night.

That is the agony of

Waiting…

Waiting…

Waiting…

LOVE LOST

I understand that you don't love me

anymore.

I have no problem with that.

You have the right to

love whom you will.

You count too, you know.

What I want means nothing unless

you want it too.

The thing that gives me the problem is:

Why do you have to keep tearing

my wound open?

When I start to heal, there you are.

not only tearing it open, but

rubbing salt and my nose in it too.

I love you still, you know that.

But I can't tell

which is stronger,

the love or the pain.

Walking away sounds so much easier

than it is to do.

Turning my back would require strength

of which I have so little.

Out of pain stems strength and growth,

I thank God for growth

or this would

All be for nothing.

LOW SELF-ESTEEM

When I saw you with her

I became

Too fat

Too tall

Too dark

Hair too nappy

Hips too big

Feet too.

Nose too wide

Lips too thick

Just plain ugly

that's me

Just plain ugly

ETERNITY

The color of you

spinning its magical web

like a million sunsets all

wrapped into one.

My insides reach out

to touch, to feel,

to incite a riot

at the center of your being.

Burning, smoke of desire

embers refueled daily.

burn without shame,

knowing it burns in return.

The emptiness of days gone

no longer haunt my

every move.

Emptiness is full,

filled with the motion of

time moving forward,

toward that endless place

called eternity

IN MEMORY

You left this place, and went somewhere else.

I sure pray that you are with God.

I never really got to know you.

We didn't spend that

kind of time.

I really wish I had taken the time.

As close as we were

I never really knew you.

What was behind the fun and games attitude?

Did you really disregard life that much?

Who are you Mickey?

I never knew.

How does it feel to die?

What does it feel like to be dead?

Do you miss us?

Can you see us?

I miss you, A part of me died

when you died.

I never really understood it

It seemed so pointless

to me.

I know you weren't really happy

But that could have been worked out.

You didn't have to be so reckless

and have it all snuffed out.

I'm really angry with you Mickey.

It's no easier for me than it was for you.

But I stayed

And its really not that bad

except

you aren't

here.

THE GIFT

I am the prize

I got the stuff

And you didn't give it to me.

I got the stuff

Don't hurt no more

I got the stuff

Ran out of tearn

I got the stuff

On top of the world

I got the stuff

Blind no more

I got the stuff

Now I know

I got the stuff

I got the stuff

.

MAGIC

You walked into the room

So sauve and so cool.

All my signals yess

Danger----beware!

I ducked and I dodged

But I couldn't get out

Of the way.

How I tried,

I didn't want to

But the magnetic force

Kept sucking, pulling

Me closer and closer

I didn't want to

I just couldn't help myself

You could have been a magician

Cause you sure had

The magic touch.

Your eyes,

They hypnotized me

I tried to turn away

But I couldn't break the trance.

Do you remember me

Like I remember you?

I can still feel your heartbeat.

We didn't have to talk.

I sat between your legs,

Leaned back on your chest

And listened to your heartbeat

And we communicated.

What happened?

I didn't end it and

Neither did you.

We simply

Stopped.

PURPLE MEMORIES

Webs of desire

spun on the telephone.

Rushing, needing

wanting, desiring

getting.

Closeness, touch.

Deeply penetrating me

with your eyes.

Bring back the life

that was long dead.

Revival, Ressurrection.

Erection.

Billowing whitness

beneath me.

Golden blackness

above me.

Peiercing, penetrating,

meeting, sending,

going.

Redness meets blackness.

Ecstacy.

Cirlces, pulling,

calling.

Minds blown.

Stereotypes broken.

Billowing whitness

beneath me.

Golden blackness

above me.

Loving

Sinking

Purple Memories.

Plush and Thick.

Rich, promising.

Purple memories

Staying.

Imbedded.

Blown Minds

of Purple Memories

A TRIBUTE TO MOREHOUSE HIGH

As I write this, it's homecoming season for most high schools and I feel sad. I feel a sadness that won't leave. A longing for Morehouse High. My thoughts race as I go back, back to another time and space.

Whoosh, two points, James "Boo" Wilson. Everybody knows I've had a crush on "Boo" since fifth grade.

I was so excited, I made Varsity Cheerleader. Gold felt skirt and blue knit sweater. Blue and gold pom pom's.

Hey Gang! Hey Gang!

BLUE AND GOLD.

"Blue and gold forever,

Great team they are,

Yell for the Tigers,

The best by far."

I remember the big "Blue Bird" with the tiger on the side. The gold tiger. Morehouse Tigers, yelling out the windows, "We won."

Hey Gang! Hey Gang!

MIGHTY TIGERS

"Oh, we're the Mighty Tigers

Oh yes we are."

Morehouse was a very special school, in a very special time, in a very special town, Bastrop, Louisiana. Bastrop is in Morehouse Parish. It's a Paper Mill town in Northern Louisiana, just sigh of the Arkansas border. The thing that makes Bastrop so special is the paper mill. This town is one of those that you don't have to pass through to get to anywhere "important." Without the mill, no one would even know Bastrop is there. You always knew when you were within miles of Bastrop because it smelled like the whole town "passed gas" in unison. The mill and the pulp ditch did that.

Hey Gang! Hey Gang!

END, CENTER, TACKLE GUARD.

"End, Center, Tackle, Guard.

Hit your man and

Hit him hard.

Hit him high,

Hit him low.

Come on Morehouse,

Let's go."

The special time was a time of "Separate, But Equal" schools. Maybe not equal, but definitely separate. It was a time when we knew who we were, where we were going and how we would get there. Morehouse was a "colored" school and later a Black school. I wonder if any of us appreciated that we were Black and we were together back then. Did we appreciate our ability to be natural? No pretense, no hiding, just being ourselves. Did we appreciate the special care and attention our teacher gave us? Did we appreciate having nothing to prove, no whites to impress or compete with? I miss that time of innocence and freedom.

Hey Gang! Hey Gang!

PUSH 'EM BACK

"Push 'em back,

Shove 'em back,

Any way you get 'em back."

The campus was beautiful. Morehouse was built in stages. Some of the buildings were old wooden ones, some were brick and new. There were tall pine trees all around, a playground, real concrete sidewalks, dirt paths, gravel parking lots and grassy knolls.

The campus housed elementary, junior high and high school grades. The trek to school each morning was a major event. Few of us rode the big yellow busses with "Morehouse Parish Training Schools" painted on the sides. Most of us walked to school, from near and far. There was an array of activities going on during the walk. Big kids teasing the little ones. Little boys chunking rocks at the girls they liked. First graders and seniors walking together. Whole families going to school together. Stopping at Mr. Daniel's hangout on the way to and from school for a quick dance.. Boys stopped to harmonize for a while and the girls stopped to listen.

My mother didn't allow me to go to Mr. Daniel's hangout, but I went anyway. IF she showed up looking for me, everyone just made a big circle and I squatted down in the middle until she left. On any day during the week , between August and May, at 7:30 a.m., you could see a rainbow of color, walking toward grand old Morehouse High.

Hey Gang! Hey Gang!

M-O-R-E

"M-O-R-E

H-O-U-S-E,

Morehouse, Morehouse,

We're gonna win

This game tonight!"

The words rattle around in my head with no place to set them down. Tiger Stadium. Tiger Sweetheart. Miss Morehouse. Did I dream Morehouse or did it really happen?

Principal Jimmie Smith. Principal Henry V. Adams. Special men, loving men, caring men. But when I was in elementary school, I hated Mr. Adams through no fault of his own.

Every morning I tried to get in an extra few minutes sleep before starting my day and Mama would come into my room and say, "Professor Adams said, 'Haul it out'."

I remember riding on the back of the big white Cadillac convertible with Alice Burrell and Edrie Williams in the Cotton Festival Parade. Melvin Dixon convinced me to enter the "Miss Cotton" contest. Melvin was always convincing me to do something when he wasn't performing in one of Mr. Twymon's award winning plays.

I didn't win the Miss Cotton contest, but I was a runner up. It was a team effort. Mrs. Naomi Smith arched my eyebrows, showed me how to shave under my arms and did my makeup. Johnnie Mae Jackson loaned me her brand new white bathing suit. My best friend didn't have enough money to attend the competition but "Boo" Wilson was on the door and let her peek. I sang Mary Wells', "Two Lovers" for the talent competition. I was so nervous but I got through it My dress was lilac. It was perfect for my dark skin. It didn't matter that I had worn it earlier for my piano recital or that I would wear it later for the prom. We didn't have a lot of money for that sort of thing. Ivory Joe Hunter was at the coronation and sang to us. He even danced with us too.

Hey Gang! Hey Gang!

TWO BITS.

"Two bits, four bits,

Six bits, a dollar.

All for Morehouse,

Stand up and holler."

Do you remember just before Miss Moore and Mr. Strickland got married, how they thought we didn't know they were dating? How we all had to act surprised when they announced their engagement?

I REMEMBER...........................

......Mrs. Debose's quiet eyes. Did you know you taught me to cook. Mama never allowed me to cook when I was growing up, you gave me my only chance in the kitchen. I'm pretty good too.

......Mrs. Twymon's stately beauty. Did you know you were the first to tell me I can write? Do you still say, "That will never do?"

......Mr. Fitch's cool stroll. Do you still walk with your hands in your pockets, jingling your coins? You were the first cool person I ever saw. In my nine year old eyes everyone else paled next to you. I'd never seen anybody like you.

......Coach Washington's stern stare, "Mr. Serious" Do you still watch over the Morehouse campus with the love and attention you always gave it?

......Mrs. Washington's gentle beauty. Are you still grooming girls to become gracious ladies?

......Mrs. Maria Cain's loving encouragement. If there are any lost, lonely children in heaven, I'm sure you've found them by now.

......Coach Payne's slow drawl. Are you still helping young men become they best they can be?

......Marvin Butler, young, wonderful, Marvin Butler. Are you still getting into as much trouble as you used to?

......Mr. Reese and Mr. Alexander cramming math down our throats. Thank you sirs for loving us that much.

......Mrs. Boughton trying to control the class. Are you still yelling, "Pay attention?"

I REMEMBER......

......Gwen Crowder and I with our heads together sharing secrets, talking about Enoch Hubbard and Otis Bush.

......Watching the band do the "Florida" and nobody could "Florida" like Kenny "Pete" Anderson.

......Doll Baby strutting her stuff in front of the band. Beautiful skin, glistening in the sun. A pretty Black woman.

......Leo "Satchmo" Richardson twirling his trumpet, doing the "Florida" back. Everyone on their feet, yelling, screaming.

......Long, lanky, Willie Bowie. So shy and yet so handsome. He didn't know it though.

......Dances in the gym. The Texas Hop, the Mashed Potatoes, the Madison, the Continental Walk, the Slop, the Sookie, the Wobble.

I REMEMBER......

......Roosevelt "Black Diamond" Jackson, Bettie Jones, Horace Mitchell, Willie Payne, Joe Payne, Sidney Wilson, Johnny Fred Harris, Shirley Long, Melba Jean White, Aileen Graham, Ed Manago, Benoni Cherry, Jesse Stephenson, Betty Ward, Shirley Jackson, Thomas Carter, Smith Jackson, Lee Jackson Woods, Maxine Keys, Betty Utsey, Joe David Whitmore, James Hall.

We separated, went our separate ways. Detroit, Chicago, Milwaukee, Dallas, Houston, Los Angeles, Oakland, Baton Rouge, New Orleans, New York, Cleveland and yes, even Bastrop. We promised each other that we'd return to Morehouse's hallowed halls some day.

But alas, something happened. We got lost in the shuffle, slipped through the cracks. Where did we go wrong? What happened? Desegregation happened and Morehouse was no more. They tell me Union is gone too. That's not the way we planned it. I feel like a person with a country. Desegregation with all it's promise left a gaping hole an impassible chasm, an un-rightable wrong. Someone got rid of Morehouse. Someone changed her name. It's something else now, a desegregated junior high school.

I feel cheated. I'll never be able to go to another Morehouse homecoming game. I'll never be able to stand up as an alumna. I'll never have the privilege of being a Booster. Where do we go at reunion time? Where is our common ground? How will we keep our long ago promises to each other? Will we ever meet again?

Desegregation seemed so promising but it stole so much. It robbed us of Morehouse, our past. Another part of our history gone forever. Of all the things I've lost in life, I miss Morehouse the most.

Morehouse High, our Alma Mater, you loved us and we loved you. That can never be taken away.

Hey Gang! Hey Gang!

ALMA MATER

"Hail to our Alma Mater!

Dear is her name

and there shall be no other

to surpass her fame.

Hers is the hand that guides us,

day after day.

And we shall stand

beside her as we

go on our way.

May blessings be upon her,

Shepherd of youth.

She holds the seat of honor,

in the hall of truth.

Memories of her shall never

fade from our hearts.

And we shall praise her ever,

For the love she imparts."

www.ingramcontent.com/pod-product-compliance
Lightning Source LLC
Chambersburg PA
CBHW020513100426
42813CB00030B/3222/J